In Code

IN CODE

POEMS BY

Maryann Corbett

ABLE MUSE PRESS

Able Muse Press

www.ablemusepress.com

Library of Congress Cataloging-in-Publication Data

Names: Corbett, Maryann, author.
Title: In Code : Poems / Maryann Corbett.
Description: San Jose, CA : Able Muse Press, 2020.
Identifiers: LCCN 2020000738 (print) | LCCN 2020000739 (ebook) | ISBN 9781773490533 (paperback) | ISBN 9781773490984 (hardcover) | ISBN 9781773490540 (digital)
Subjects: LCGFT: Poetry.
Classification: LCC PS3603.O7323 I5 2020 (print) | LCC PS3603.O7323 (ebook) | DDC 811/.6--dc23
LC record available at https://lccn.loc.gov/2020000738
LC ebook record available at https://lccn.loc.gov/2020000739

Cover image: "Historically Architecture" by Lutz Peter

Cover & book design by Alexander Pepple

Maryann Corbett photo (page 79) by Mims Photography

Able Muse Press is an imprint of *Able Muse:* A Review of Poetry, Prose & Art—at

www.ablemuse.com

Able Muse Press
467 Saratoga Avenue #602
San Jose, CA 95129

code, n.

1 : a systematic statement of a body of law, especially : one given statutory force

2 : a system of principles or rules, *moral code*

3   a : a system of signals or symbols for communication

b : a system of symbols (such as letters or numbers) used to represent assigned and often secret meanings

c : coded language : a word or phrase chosen in place of another word or phrase in order to communicate an attitude or meaning without stating it explicitly

—Merriam-Webster.com

Acknowledgments

My grateful acknowledgments go to the editors of the following publications where these poems, some in earlier versions, first appeared:

Able Muse: "Polling Place" (from "Judgments"); *Alabama Literary Review*: "A Volume of Cases," "The Vanished"; *The Arkansas International*: "An Ancient in First-Year Greek"; *The Baltimore Review*: "State Office Building, Seventh Floor"; *The Barefoot Muse*: "Saturday Edition"; *Berfrois*: "An Orientation," "Map of the Ten Thousand Countries of the World," "Police Procedural"; *Columba*: "A Room at the Student Union"; *Dappled Things*: "Seven Little Poems about Making Laws"; *The Evansville Review*: "The Indexers Talk Back to Borges"; *First Things*: "Experimental Design"; *Fourteen by Fourteen*: "Hamartia"; *Innisfree Poetry Journal*: "Spotter Observations"; *Life and Legends*: "Resolve"; *LIGHT*: "Earworm Studies"; *Literary Imagination*: "'The best lack all conviction'," "December 1399"; *Literary Matters*: "Sleep, Loss," "Wildfire Season"; *Measure Review*: "Fugue in October"; *Mezzo Cammin*: "An Aisle of Japanese Tree Lilacs," "Aubade for the Old Houses," "Silent Partner"; *Modern Poetry in Translation*: "Riddle 40: Pen in Hand," "Riddle 52 : Ballista"; *The New Verse News*: "Fearful for my government job, dreaming of retirement, I think of Du Fu," "Following the News, We Return You to Music of the Season," "Song for the Shooters"; *One*: "*Myristica fragrans*"; *Pangyrus*: "The Nutshell Studies of Unexplained Death"; *The Panhandler*: "Apparition at University and Park" (as "News Flash"), "Working Draft"; *PN Review*: "Creed," "A Diplomatic Post," "Threats"; *Poets Reading the News*: "Universal Vault Fire, 1 June 2008"; *Potomac Review*: "New Media"; *Presence*: "Praise Ode to the Customer Service Agent"; *The Raintown Review*: "Ninety Seconds of News Coverage at 6 P.M.," "Refuting Marvell";

The Rotary Dial: "Open Verdict," "Poses," "Schema"; *The Saint Paul Almanac*: "A Duty"; *The San Diego Reader*: "Concealed Carry," "Lesson"; *Snakeskin*: "Reassessment," "True Crime"; *Tampa Review*: "Unexplained Bagpipes"; *Terrain*: "Reasons for Hesitation"; *Thrush*: "The Forgery"; *Tipton Poetry Journal*: "Stone Ground"; *Umbrella*: "A Personal Account"; *Water~Stone Review*: "In Code"

"A Volume of Cases" appeared in *Mid Evil* (University of Evansville Press, 2015).

"Creed" appeared on *Poetry Daily*.

"Hamartia" appeared in the chapbook *Dissonance* (Scienter Press, 2009).

"Saturday Edition" appeared in the anthology *Irresistible Sonnets* (Headmistress Press, 2014).

"The Vanished" appeared in *The Orison Anthology, Vol 2* (Orison Books, 2017).

Thanks are also due to my former colleagues in the Office of the Revisor of Statutes of the Minnesota Legislature. They taught me volumes, over almost thirty-five years, about the law, about the intricacies of lawmaking, and about the foibles of the Legislature's members, while allowing me to lecture them about the need to shorten their sentences. For their patience and their friendship, I am very grateful.

And as always, I owe a debt of gratitude to the members, moderators, and administrators of *Eratosphere*, past and present, who helped some of these poems along.

Contents

In Code

Threats

Attention barks the voice out of the speaker
and once again *Attention*, and our fingers
peck-peck, close documents, log off devices,
grab coats, yank at the bags we schlep our lives in.
A threat has been reported in this building.

Who on this skyblue April day believes it?
Not the last holdouts, sitting there, still screen-glued,
peering round-shouldered at the tasks before them.
The voice squawks orders, end-stopped, razor-edgy.
We file outdoors to our assigned location.

Was there a warning at the Murrah building?
None. Only the rage of the explosion
monstrously heard at fifty-five miles distant.
That was an April day. The sun was shining,
the wounded building gaping in the daylight.
The children bleeding in the arms of firemen.

But not here, not today. Today, some foul-up—
a fault of wiring? burnt toast in the break room?—
has sprung us, laughing here among pink roses
and petals drifting from the flowering crab trees.

Something could happen, yes. We know things happen.
We have our work, our lives, for the time being.

State Office Building, Seventh Floor

For the night teams at the Revisor's Office

The building lifts the bank of lighted windows
into the darkness.

Approach on any night in spring—late April
into mid-May—
and there it is, hung in the night, reciting
still here, still here.

Lit windows always mean a late shift, working.
Up there, all night,
they work. They make the bills and the amendments
ready for morning.

Think of the weariness of old lighthouses
on the North Shore.
Think of the concentration of the surgeons
in trauma units.

Farfetched, you say? Maybe you balk at mixing
these metaphors?

The law, a tanker lighted into harbor
on a roiled sea?
Sure. Reams of paper hauled back from committee
are a beached vessel,
the wreckage of hours wrangling, the loved projects
lying in fragments—

The law as midnight lowlife, deal gone pear-shaped,
slashed, bleeding?
Up there, they reconstruct the damaged corpus
scalpel-exactly.

Late, very late, they work by the lit windows.
No loud suspense film
lauds them. No documentary explains them.

They are profoundly
ignorable. My one task is to prod you
to think about them.

Seven Little Poems about Making Laws

i Prayer by the chaplain:
cloudy pleas, made to a god
we keep nebulous.

ii Farmers' Lobby Week:
seed-hatted, they plow the halls
sowing their concord.

iii Sulfite pages in
early casebooks flake to crumbs.
So much for the past.

iv (Oh dear. There are now
seven hundred sixty words
in this subitem.)

v Where white silk brocade
covers the tall, formal walls,
we cut food support.

vi Capitol café:
German proverbs, whitewashed since
1917,

vii are restored to view
with bright applause. Old hatreds
have new objects now.

An Aisle of Japanese Tree Lilacs

North lawn, State Office Building

We amble from the train
or from our cars, far off, resigned to lesser lots.
The great, with the bespoke, ramp-covered parking spots,
who enter from low-ceilinged, dank concrete,
miss this last sweet: white-petalled, fragrant rain.

Floret and bract and spray
above the formal walk's procession to the entryway
toss celebration like a ticker-tape parade
hailing all comers—
the stony-faced in pinstripes, staid,
equally with the fashion-backward slummers,
the rumpled and the sleek,
clandestine poet, closet rocker, gambler on a winning streak,
the garrulous, the oddly blessèd meek.

Arched by a triumph cheered in flowering trees,
like generals in old Rome,
we're conquerors by a bald truth: here we come
out of our war-zone mornings and our muddled histories
into these ordered, honorific spaces.
We swipe our key cards, breathe once, step inside,
and set our working faces.

Fugue in October

Baroque chamber ensemble and homeless encampment, Saint Paul

Perfect: the singers, strings, and keyboards. Perfect

> Bruised sky above the tents of the squatters' district

the little jewel-box church, its bright acoustic

> calm in the year's last mildness, the only music

softened a little in the candles' lighting,

> the mumbling underpass. The wind. No fighting

for this is God's mind, woven of harmonies

> for once. Tonight, for once, no one ODs—

and our souls thread through the flame of the vigil lamp

> someone got lucky at the entrance ramp

as we hold, hold to Monteverdi's line

> (panhandling, on this warm day, with a sign)

and stop our breath until the last string dies

and parcels out his manna of salty fries

in the last great chord of his *Beatus vir*

while sirens wail some sorrow, far from here

Poses

State Capitol mall

Step off the train and there it is: the statue,
bronze and bombastic. Even before you see
the white Cass Gilbert dome, it looms: the statue,
larger-than-life Leif Erikson, that statue
of wishful thinking. Largely, it's a lie—
that winged helmet, for instance—but then, statues
are not about *verismo*. A good statue,
like a good eulogy, recasts the truth.
The furrowed, wind-scrubbed Scandinavian truth,
the debt-drowned farms, melt down into this statue,
its nobly bearded chin lifted to freedom
or some such resonant word. And here's the dome

next left: the Capitol, squaring off with the dome
of the Cathedral. Strung between them, statues
stud the green mall. No tree, no shrub is random:
it's a stage set for certitude, all kingdom,
power, and glory. Stroll downhill. You see
(staring back at the wedding cake of dome)
the gilt Roman quadriga, flashy as stardom.
Here Floyd Olson harangues you silently
in green patina. Farther downhill lie
man-and-boy Lindberghs—earthbound—that belie
their troubled end. There's Humphrey, speechless. Truth
is difficult to learn from art. But truth

10

is, these are tourists; would they want the truth?
The sculptor understands. Thus it is seldom
that public art admits the messier truths.
Yet here: the war memorials. Their truth
seeps from the slick black granite. Their one statue—
a flat, bronze void, a cutout—wails the truth
out of its absence, straining at a truth
that jars the still air, yelling *Heresy!*
When they are dead who lived this, who will see
the smoldering contradictions of the truth
in these plain shapes, and who will give the lie
to this bright polish? speak to the Old Lie

candidly, calmly, waiting for reply?
Who will unslant the canted textbook truth?
Which of the age-old warnings will apply?
No answer. The unspeaking bronzes lie
out in all weathers. Their mild clemency
turns Gettysburg, the Somme, the Bulge, My Lai,
the unnamed nightmares as they multiply,
to dumb abstraction. In that light, a statue
settles into forgetting. Such a statue
deadens against the pain and finally,
stripped clean of truth, is beautiful. To see
this is a sort of peace. A sort of mercy.

Look back; take in the vista. What you see—
the sweep of green, the tulip beds, the lie
of bronzes in their burnished courtesy—
is pure Platonic form. Democracy
as dream. Memory purged. Unvarnished truth

creeps in at dawn, where tourists never see
brown hands mowing, or sniff the piquancy
of fresh manure on rose beds. Though the dome
brays its old songs, *imperium* and serfdom,
it's all an outlook. All in how you see.
See there: teachers, unflappable as statues,
herd their unruly charges past the statues.

Where can they learn pure silence but from statues,
these field-trip children, crazed with spring and boredom,
swarming the lawns and gleaming steps? Now see
them pose for pictures: glossy, colored lies
parents will cling to, though they know the truth.

The Forgery

1. The painting he brought you:

   (a) was a standard religious motif, the Scourging at the Pillar

   (b) bore, in its concocted provenance, the name of a lost Caravaggio

   (c) disturbed you with the memory of your Catholic-school childhood, in which you found yourself aroused by images of the stripped Savior, the cloth loose at his hips

2. You knew the work was genuine because:

   (a) the signature had all the authentic features, and chemical analysis dated the canvas to the correct period

   (b) the seller spoke softly, had white hair, and wore a Roman collar, and the paleness of his eyes unnerved you

   (c) in that chiaroscuro was a darkness you deeply knew, and a light you were unsure of

3. You lost your faith in it when:

   (a) minute traces of titanium, impossible for the date, turned up in more sensitive assays, and the artist cursed a mislabeled tube of lead white

(b) you heard in dreams the Allegri *Miserere*, the little glass
   voices of the sopranos broken with pain

4. The painting still hangs in your hallway because:

   (a) you are ashamed to remember what it cost you

   (b) you feel on the skin of your own shoulders the scourge of
      an old hope

   (c) you stepped, years ago, into its frame and can never return

Map of the Ten Thousand Countries of the World

*Matteo Ricci, 1602. Woodblock prints on paper. Exhibited at
the Minneapolis Institute of Arts.*

All the inhabitants are excellent.
       —*Map notation on present-day America, as translated
         from the Chinese*

We are the excellent inhabitants.
We conjure maps within a glowing screen
and in our chariot pulled by its own power
travel to see a map.
                    In carpeted silence,
the six great woodblock panels span the wall,
dense with *zhongwen*, crosshatch, wriggling inks.
Inscrutable, but for the quiet aid
of dry-mount signs that offer us translations.

Like Ricci—in the robes of a Confucian,
serene among the sages, missionary
eager to teach the faith of the Lord of Heaven—
the map sets out the world's wild variousness:

> *Patagonia, kingdom of the giants,*
> *inhabitants not more than ten feet high. . . .*

> *The land of dwarves, its one-foot men and women*
> *constantly devoured by hawks and cranes. . . .*

And in the lower right, the universe,
the sun, the moon, the planets' epicycles,
the perfect Earth unmoving at the center.

The sages, with their great intelligence,
grasped at once the power of this knowledge.
(So Ricci tells us in his own great book.)

We excellent inhabitants squint to read.
Dazzled amid the folds of glossy handouts,
we thread our way out of the thousand galleries,
returning home by signs, believing signs.

> *No one here indulges in superstition*
> *but all adhere to the faith of the Lord of Heaven,*

and so we seat ourselves before the screen
to let our minds be silent, satisfied
the world in all its truth now lies before us.

The Nutshell Studies of Unexplained Death

*Crime scene dioramas created as teaching tools by Frances
Glessner Lee*
—Renwick Gallery, Washington, DC

Well-behaved voyeurs
bend above these exquisite
dollhouse miniatures

where the small-scale poor
die in '40s dailiness.
Blood speckles a floor

tiled in one-to-twelve
scale. Ditto bath fixtures, beds,
plates shocked from a shelf.

Here's a girl's sliced neck.
Here's another, legs jutting
from a tub, freaklike.

Is this Dresden head
brush-tipped with the purpling
livor of the dead?

To appreciate
such intently crafted pain,
one must contemplate

finger-cramping care:
quarter-inch-high postcards, penned
with a single hair.

A close eye for sin's
rigor vitae: tiny socks
hand-knitted with pins.

Strict detail is key.
Look there for the rage of God.
Search for that and see,

sisters. As will I,
taken with the pains by which
quiet women die.

Open Verdict

They interviewed her office mate.
He groped for insights, which were small.
I didn't know her well, he said.
Nice girl, but unremarkable.

The self coworkers thought they knew
seemed pleasant, laughed its well-bred laugh,
billed hours and planned vacation trips,
smiled for the annual photograph,

but left a stable office job
abruptly, as though forced to flee
by demons draped in chalk-stripe gray
cloaks of invisibility

over their asset-column souls.
Were any of them actual friends?
Nobody says exactly that.
She turned her key card in.
                           There ends

the evidence we have. The life
stops leaving traces. No report;
no missing person.
                 In the kitchen,
food was years beyond its date

and moldy dishes filled the sink
the day they came to seize the flat
and found the skeleton, before
the sightless television set.

Spotter Observations

All morning the news
     goes south,
geese mobilizing
     abaft
a leader's bluster.
     The sky
rumpled camouflage.

     No clear
outlook for these days.

Following the News, We Return You to Music
of the Season

And as the alto line shoulders its ache
of dissonance against the calm soprano,
I think, Always the same *mysterium*:

the moment when at last the milk-drunk infant
droops against the breast, and the new mother
sighs into sleep, is darkened by the knowledge
that soldiers from a foreign empire are quartered
in the next street, while a strongman in the hills
clings to his shreds of power. When he strikes,
we wake to scenes of the bloody slaughter of children.

For them there are few carols, rarely sung.

> *Peshawar*
> *28 December 2014*
> *Feast of the Holy Innocents*

New Media

No horn-rimmed lone intoner now. No grand
paterfamilias of evening news
shepherding watchers soberly toward views
moderate, monochrome, subdued, and bland.
Instead, kaleidoscopes! Mad movement crammed
down every microsecond. Wizards' brews
of weird conspiracy. Passions cut loose
in danse-macabre musics of the damned
that dun a ceaseless reverb in the skull,
hissing permission: *Feed the fire of your fear.*
Enrobe yourself in judgment, its long pall
swaddling you tight. Declare that you despise.
Lean on your narrow life as on a prayer.
Believe your barefaced heart, knowing it lies.

Apparition at University and Park

That talking head haloed in golden curls—
the one I see in every night's devotions
to the gods of local news—is here, in flesh.
Here, in a body like mine (too short, too shapeless),
the oracle whose one word conjures tempests
in the political teapot where I work
is peering at traffic, waiting to cross at the light,
Hermès scarf no longer neatly tucked
at the collar, Prada jacket hanging askew.
And though she is followed at a reverent distance
by acolytes bearing cameras and lighting equipment,
her lipsticked mouth, red as blood sacrifice,
droops at the corners. Her face is not lit by news
of campaign money, out-of-town liaisons,
or DUI convictions, not transformed
by the god into the Sybil. Mortal, merely.

Decency seems to require that I look away.

Unexplained Bagpipes

After reading that white-supremacist marches are often led by pipers

A skewer through the ear,
it spits you to the spot
until you suss it out.
It's unexpected here:

back garden, mid-Midwest
midsummer, -week, and -day.
Ripping the aural chintz
of airborne oldies airplay,

it groans a jaunty grind.
The kids turn cartwheels, smitten.
The sound itself has forgotten
the quarrel it trawls around.

Garish, clownish, bizarre,
still blocks away, it hauls
over your ivied walls
the rack-nerve rumor of war.

Work now. Gather the spent,
blood-spattered peonies.
Daylilies crowd the fence,
desperate. Like refugees.

After the Political Speeches

I have done it again. I do it over and over.

Again, again, I steel myself to endure it—
to sit on the living-room couch, handing my heart
across the screen, into those whirligig
orator-arms, where tongues like juggled cutlery
mince the meat of my thought and serve my brains
back to my own mouth on a silver platter
(Colonial vintage, cast by Paul Revere)
with bread to feed five thousand, and a side of circus.

Don't I remember how, before it's over,
somebody's always poisoned, choked, garroted?
How the dish curdles in a sauce of *sang-des-martyrs?*

But here is my gut, growling for what it lacks,
and this odd goulash, honeyed to taste like justice.

Again, starving and desperate, I gulp it down.

Ninety Seconds of News Coverage at 6 P.M.

Media in armadas mass,
poised to pounce where the committee
titans will emerge and pass.
(Camera lighting has no pity.)

Winners, in the highbeam glare,
blaze blue-suited, repp-tied, virile.
(Losers with a hangdog air
slink to find their corners, feral.)

Staff, impartial, rustle by,
whispering toward the snack machine,
silent with the mystery
confidential eyes have seen.

In an empty gallery space,
a lobbyist whose face I know
pokes his cell phone, poker faced.
(He was Speaker, years ago.)

Under skies as blank as God,
awkward limestone fragments fall
from the classical facade
crumbling off the Capitol.

Saturday Edition

Page one, above the fold: the world in flames.
A luxury hotel gapes like a sore.
In mammoth type, the headlines yell the names
of prophets stoking hells of holy war.

In Business, meanwhile, there is calm discussion
of sales rates for the sexy underclothes
pitched by Victoria's Secret, and a fashion
for surgical revision of the nose.

It isn't news to those who sell the paper:
their readers can take only so much hell.
They proffer me the surgeon and the draper
as pastures where my bovine brain may dwell,

ignoring, while it chews on this confection,
the screams of children from the other section.

Wildfire Season

Iliad 2.455–457
    —With thanks to A.E. Stallings

. . . Just as a lightning strike,
or a stray spark, or some such randomness
takes hold, sudden as thought, of a wildland ridge
so that we see, in distances and news clips,
tall tonguings of molten saffron-orange
lick hugely from one hillside to another
and plumes of ashy black, poufs and bouffants
lifting, then sifting down in crumbs of grit
on the attendant rich suburban houses
where families listen nervously for updates—
which highways will be glutted with sedans,
and Range Rovers, and SUVs, gut-stuffed
with people in flight, angry and disbelieving
that a random flash or spark could wrest from them
the lovely form and matter of their lives,
leaving not even gods to blame, just so. . . .

Schema

It was lovely at first. He was kindness itself on the phone
and his beautiful plans had the purity of the sincere,
with their well-tempered goals, and their vision so artlessly clear
that I had to believe, though I thought he should work it alone.

And it worked like a charm. Little envelopes came. They were mailed
from that address in Zurich and plump with those generous checks.
We were happy, and glory rolled in from one week to the next.
And it worked while it worked. It succeeded! At least, till it failed.

The accountant informs me that all of the money's gone west,
which is sad, and it sours the taste of a years-long affair.
It's a medium-security prison. I write to him there
and I miss him, but really, in orange he's not at his best.

Silent Partner

Welcome, newcomer to this vital project.
Dismiss the stares, the envious sidelong glances.
For what we have in mind, your skills are perfect.

Grace without flaw, discretion without defect:
they've taught you the smooth moves of these old dances.
You grasp that gossip's tainted, small talk suspect,

and rightly timed, a smile will change the subject.
(That younger man who looks at you askance is
no one important.) Bear in mind the prospect

of quiet advancement. Trust, trust is your object.
Wait for a dreamer wafting through his trances,
moth to the flame of a sympathetic affect,

Legion his name. The misfit, yes; the reject.
Loners, whiners, beggars for cash advances,
the bitter exes, the sad sacks, the henpecked—

but mind you never lose that cheerful aspect!
(If someone ends in dodgy circumstances,
you'll know to swat the knowledge like an insect.)

Handshake agreement, yes. No written contract.
This is the apple; bite and take your chances.
The words you never speak are always perfect.

A Duty

The light this morning, charging across the river and up Saint Peter Street as if no doubt were possible.

The twenty stories of the building. The vertical columns, window and black spandrel, aimed at heaven in a dream of the Gothic ideal. Uprightness. The guidebook says, "American Perpendicular."

Security, gray and resigned. The scanners where I lay down my pursed and briefcased life. Where I raise my arms to be wanded, as if I could be proved worthy of trust. Then: the sudden opulent hall. Three stories of polished marble, jet black walls, blinding white floor, mirrored ceiling.

At the end of the colonnade, the *Indian God of Peace*, hulking in thirty-eight feet of Mexican white onyx. A memorial, the Great War. The placard says, "a vision in the smoke of their peace pipes."

The elevator doors, sculpted bronze in the iconography of the WPA. Slave, Indian, farmer, factory worker, each in his place. Inside, when I turn around: big '30s floor-buttons. An antique mechanism.

On floor fifteen now, the flawless wood panels sheathe the walls, their hand-rubbed depth a luxury bought Depression-cheap. The sober oak of benches where I squirm.

Voir dire, a phrase in Anglo-Norman. Telling the truth in a dead tongue. The badge I wear reads JUROR in dignified dark blue. When I leave the courtroom and approach a group in the hallway, a blank drops over their conversation.

In the great hall at leave-taking, the pleasantries, as if this were pleasant. My white face reflected, black, from the marble walls. Black and white, as if anything were.

Saint Paul City Hall and Ramsey County Courthouse, design by Ellerbe & Co., 1932

True Crime

You understand it's not like CSI.
Right? says the judge. She pulls her glasses down
and glares. The jurors smirk and look away,

thinking, *Well, duh*: no babe or hunky guy
is anywhere in evidence. The clown
who's Plaintiff is in ripped jeans and a tee;

the prosecutor's suit is thin and shiny.
His line is that Defendant pulled a gun
on Plaintiff, on a stretch of rural highway,

but photos (staged) to show what P. could see
look wrong: a different car, a different weapon,
a trumped-up view not shown convincingly—

no fingerprints, no blood, no DNA.
Only the troopers' word they found the gun.
(The tech can't get their video to play.)

And why they thought the accused should testify
is still a mystery. But the jury's keen
to take the case and wrangle. What they say

can't apprehend what's true and what's a lie:
which actor here's the *sympathetic* one?
Drama at last: men shout and women cry.

The state will try again another day.
Jury dismissed. No justice will be done
this episode. It's not like CSI.

Song for the Shooters

"Somehow this has become routine"
—*Barack Obama,* Washington Post, *1 October 2015*

How this became routine, no one can tell.
The bashful toddler's ringlet-clouded head,
how early did it learn the song of hell?

The nattering of talking heads, so shrill
it bored into the childish mind and bred?
How is this now routine? No one can tell.

The silent, brooding boys who tripped and fell
down through the blacklight labyrinth of dread
whose only soundtrack is the song of hell?

We guess they held a hurt, its heft, its chill,
and gripped a fury till their fingers bled—
routine, routine. This little we can tell:

post office, movie theater, shopping mall,
and schoolroom whence all innocence is fled
ring with the wretched antiphons of hell.

What love, ringing its changes on the knell
of cell phones from the pockets of the dead,
must hear *routine, routine*? No one can tell
how human ears unhear the song of hell.

Police Procedural

The requisite three murder plots unsnarled,
red herrings snuffled, ragged subplots snipped,
and cottage-garden placidness restored
in onscreen England and our armchair minds,
I shamble to the door for the night's lockup

and halt, knifed in the eye by mystery.

Dead ahead from the doorway, cop-car strobes,
ice-white, and the walloping reds and blues of lightbars
silhouette the burly shapes of men
(holsters and nightsticks briefly clear enough)
as they handcuff a third, more fragile-looking man,
his shoulders hunched against the might of the law.
Gnashing engines scumble other sounds.
All meanings hide themselves in the violent light.

More strobes, lightbars. Their brain-befuddling sweep
flash-outlines unknown gawkers from the sidewalk
as the thin man is folded out of sight.
Now, in muscular moves, one dark police-shape
rifles through a third car, its doors and trunk
splayed open like a pinned insect; a flashlight
pokes to be sure the thing is dead. The strobes
keep stabbing. Box-shaped ciphers thud to the pavement.

How many throbbing minutes do I stand there,
the light an icepick to my understanding?
One cop-car sidles off with the thin man,
the other with his confiscated secrets.
I watch the different, steadier lights of a tow truck
that makes short work of winching his car away.

We stumble to bed, as much in the dark as ever.

Concealed Carry

Yes, any idiot might be carrying here.
No taped-up gun-ban sign, square capitals
flapping against the supermarket doors:
FOODCO BANS FIREARMS IN THESE PREMISES.
Nada. So anybody might be packing.

But aren't we always at each other's mercy?
Guileless and stubby-fingered as the toddler
who grubbed in his mother's purse and shot her dead,
we never know what triggers we might pull.

Every word, a small bomb at the roadside.
Lob the grenade of your long and placid marriage
at the gray clerk, alone again at sixty.
Grandchild-gossip—it's acid in the face
of the woman down the aisle, still empty-armed.

Even now amid the produce bins,
as Marvin Gaye wails *heard it through the grapevine*,
the man beside you is setting his broccoli down
sharply, like someone skewered through the vitals.

Earworm Studies

Research suggests that frequent earworms are correlated with anxieties and obsessive-compulsive disorder.

The studies make it clear.
Admit you're prone to them
and water-cooler Freuds start in. They'll slap you
with half the weirdo syndromes in the latest *DSM*,

swearing it's in your head,
whatever sets this off.
A verse drifts through your consciousness, and *blam!*
Spasmodic as a cough,

a needle drags across your soul's scratched vinyl
and skips. And skips. And skips.
Drilling you someplace cranial or spinal,
it teaches, with its endless audio clips,

the mode whereby the most innocuous tune
can turn a torture-screw.
A plainchant's oil and balm,
a boy soprano fluting, *All is calm . . . ,*
"YMCA," the theme from Scooby Doo—

recursive thought-balloons
that swell and pop, and swell again, and pop.
Be calm. The simplest way to make them stop
will drop in your lap like a sack of gold doubloons:

the kid writing with lipstick on a wall;
the spousal cell phone call
reporting on the sad demise of the car so lately bought;
the unpaid bill discovered in the stack—

any of these will free you. When you find
that fear and anger keep a school for clarity of mind,
you learn how dear, how dear
the silence is. And in that very thought,
the torture tune comes back

like sunrise. Like the moon,
the zodiac. It's *not* all in your head.
Living repeats itself.
What did you want instead?

An Orientation

If, in the midst of this elated day,
someone took him aside with the stern warning,
Most of your life will not be like this morning,
he'd never hear it. How—while fountains play
beside clipped lawns and walkways arched with green
maples that move to stipple white and gold
on paths he and his harried parents have strolled
laden for move-in—how could he hear? He's seen
Arcadia now, where classical facades
put a straight face on tanglements of thought,
and edgy spears of light and color, wrought
in steel and glass, look daggers at the gods.

The whole week's strewn with glittering temptations
and parti-colored parties for the eyes:
gown-sleeves aflap like tropical butterflies,
professors float along in convocations.
Some one of them, someday, and over a drink,
will show him grittier visions: Rumor. Snark.
Administrative bloat. Nowhere to park.
How only summers bless you with time to think.
How even the mind's beauties fester, vexed
by deadlines, balky software, budget hassle.
How research builds its turreted air-castle,
gorgeous for one day, rubble on the next.

But here, today, does anybody give
a bleep for realness? Let us cleave to form,
leaving him to his roommate and his dorm
and whispering, *Here's the poison. Drink and live.*

Experimental Design

This tangle of *Drosophila*, these flies
low-orbiting your wineglass and my peach
niggle a question: whether meaning lies
only in multitudes. Is *all*, not *each*,
what matters? The arcana of creation
bloom from the totting up of tiny specks
from generation unto generation
of brief lives and uncomplicated sex.
We count them, yea, we count them. Thus, they count.
In aggregate, the little meanings chime
life's answers; little dabs of data mount
to heaven in their millions at a time.
The new design of darkness to appall:
the data cloud, and not the sparrow's fall.

A Diplomatic Post

After du Bellay, Les Regrets, *LXXXVI*

Walk gravely. Keep your brows heavy as lead.
Smile gravely. Fawn; be uber-courteous.
Weigh every word, and nod a sage's head
Balancing *No, my lord,* with *My lord, yes,*

And throwing in a frequent *Ah, just so!*
Add *At your service*—makes you sound sincere.
Expound at length (as if you had a clue)
About the outcome of the current war.

There'll be a lot of hands you have to kiss.
You'll sink a lot of nonexistent wealth
Into Italian suits (yes, "when in Rome . . .").

And the great thing about a post like this?
Finally, when your wardrobe, luck, and health
All fail, they ship you skint and beardless home.

Creed

When I haul my carcass up from my creaking knees
to mumble the old form
(stubbing my tongue on the brick of a new translation)

humble me, Lord, to accept the awkward history
of these your mysteries,
a plot line tangled as the morning news,

a bitterness in the mouth. First, Constantine,
pig-headed in the face of disagreement,
yelling "Impious fool!"

And Athanasius, wily, on the run,
a glamorous bandit, sending in his thugs
to rile up orthodox riot.

Councils, anathemas, excommunications,
exiles. Seventy years of holy terror,
the violent bearing it away:

a street mob in fourth-century Alexandria
wild with joy at the news
that the emperor Constantius lay dead,

which left them free to haul out their Arian bishop
and bash him to bloody pulp
to proclaim the Son *homoousios* with the Father.

Yes, in the end they faded away, the Arians—
those pie-eyed optimists, certain
sheer plodding will could make mere man divine—

a lovely notion, suddenly dodgy-sounding
with barbarian tribes at the border
and falling across the empire, the shadow of doubt.

Judgments

Election Day, state and city races

I. Polling Place

So I stand
in the blandeur of a beige community room
        fitted in haste
with flimsy booths. How ever did the grand
        and solemn doom
of the Law cook up this taupe-and-tepid taste?

        these folding tables?
these faces zombied by the bluish tint
        of LEDs?
What happened to the noble eighth-grade fables
        of Government?
And gimcrack laminated signage? Please.

        This, after weeks
of politicians' droppings in the post!
        Hectoring months
of calls and ads! A grumpy memory speaks—
        a sort of Ghost
of Pollings Past—and says, *It meant more, once.*

But no, he's wrong.
He's listened to the manic chattering
        of the unjaded heart
I had at twenty-two, when every song
        the radios could sing
sang Peace, and Things had not quite Fallen Apart.

        So my hopes flicker,
these days, like dodgy lightbulbs. Still, I'm here
        with the scuffing line,
ready to flaunt my red *I voted* sticker
        and public cheer,
passing the child-size flag and the tacky, tacked-up sign.

II. Roster Judge

Today, I am a Norn.
Today, straitly and stringently, I have sworn
and now I guard a precinct roster, one of three
severe-haired crones, judging the mystery
of who you are. For you have suffered a sea change—
new married name, new residence, some other rich and strange
transforming—and might not be who you were.
I chant the remedies, but with each one
      your frown grows angrier.

Forms, signatures. Flurries of documents.
At last, you have a ballot in your hands—
but the ballot counter questions what you're choosing
and spits it back. Three times. Already shaken, you're refusing
my help. (Of all my flustered moves, this was the rashest,
it seems.) You rip the page up, hissing *Fascist!*
and storm out, red-faced. Dumb, I take the smudged
form to its fate. *Judge not*, sayeth the Lord,
     lest ye be judged.

III. Afterword

Maybe it makes a difference. In that year
when a vast rage had torn the whole East Coast
to sodden shreds in late autumn, I slumped
at the stove in an election's morning-after,
absently stirring breakfast. And my brain
snagged on the radio's voice, the quiet story
telling how voters in a broken city
stood stoic in the day-devouring lines.
People with shattered homes, people exploring
the strange new depth of their old powerlessness,
shivered and shuffled toward their polling places
under a lead-white sky.
                          The voice signed off.
I wept in silence into my scrambled eggs.

Lesson

Once, the child of a neighbor down the alley

    (kid just getting the hang of chubby pencils;
    mother barely a nod-and-wave acquaintance)

stopped me, urgent of eyebrows, face a puzzle,
asking, would *I* be going back to school now?

No, I chuckled, I'd had enough of schooling.

    (That left out the specifics: strings of letters
    straggling after my name; gilt-edged diplomas.)

Here's what held in my brain: the pang of grown-up
panic wringing his answer: "But you *have* to!
*Fin*ish! And find a *job*. And pay the *land*lord."
Little ears, so expert at overhearing....

    (How I handled the rest, the conversation
    turning matters around to chalk and crayons,
    memory muddles now. But the scar of knowing
    woe not meant for my ears—it's a welt, still tender.)

Hamartia

"Hamartia," though often translated as "tragic flaw," means
literally a missing of the mark, a mistake.

We listen nervously. The social worker
is here now to address the block club meeting
to talk about our neighbor: the alley lurker
who barks *You think I'm a Nazi?* if we greet him
with a wave. Who thinks we blacklist him from jobs,
steal from his house. Disheveled, unemployed,
he haunts the playgrounds and the school bus stops,
tight-jawed, unnerving as an armed grenade.

The social worker asks us to consider
how this life feels (her word is *paranoid*).
How much he suffers. How he lives in fear.
The likely end, she says, is suicide.

I think of Sophocles, of tragic error.
We learn to pity. We were born with terror.

Aubade for the Old Houses

Windows, opened to June's
seductive air, admit
this morning's ruder rhythm, an insistent
Wham and *Wham* and *Wham*:
pile drivers down the block
are banging home their point.

It's undermining mine:
my love for the loose fit
of houses century-settled, rich in ornament.
I grieve for the *grandes dames*
battered to wrack last week
where those roughhousers grunt,

a business brutishly done.
Before noon breaks a sweat,
nail guns will volley; convoys of cement
trucks will hiss and slam
their air brakes, beeping back-up,
hogging the space they want.

Like me. Like everyone
who craves a place to sit,
a place to sleep, a place to pitch a tent
for the weak flesh. The stream
of bodies swells the building boom; good luck
asking that tide to wait for your consent.

Noises grind on; I groan
awake. They're whacking flat
the birdsong chorus, gaveling their blunt
verdict. The old houses of my dreaming
drunk-stagger, and I'm dumbstruck,
shamed by my own lament.

Resolve

WHEREAS, the records tell me he was twenty
in 1965, a new, spit-polished
second lieutenant aviator; and
WHEREAS, he was a rip-snorter at flying,
an ace at all of it, the buzzing low,
the cutting close, the dodging fire, the strafing,
the dropping of (as the citations have it)
his *ordnance* with a terror-eyed precision; and
WHEREAS, the photocopied texts inform me
he was devoted and performed his duty
in keeping with the Navy's highest standards; and
WHEREAS, he neutralized his targets at
Vinh Hui, Quang Nai, and many other places
the record has not troubled to provide; and
WHEREAS, tonight he will sit at a banquet table
while others praise what the citations call
his skill, his dedication, NOW THEREFORE,
BE IT RESOLVED that, as my duty requires,
I will write words that ape these commendations,
to print on heavy paper with scroll borders,
important signatures, and raised gold seals
and to be read with pomp in candlelight
at dinner. Crabcakes, or filet mignon.
Be it resolved that I have not forgotten
the faces of his targets. They run toward me
forever, naked, screaming, flesh on fire.

Riddle 52: Ballista

From the Old English of the Exeter Book

I stand on guard   for the stash I hoard
fast in fence-wires   and filled up inside
with people's loot.   In the day's light
I'm often found spitting   spear-shaped terror.
The more you stuff me,   the steadier my speed;
My leader sees lances   lunge from my belly.
Sometimes I wolf down   dark war-weapons,
the bitter points   of their poisoned barbs.
The guts inside me   are good, the lovely
cache in my innards   precious to armies.
Men remember   what comes from my mouth.

December 1399

"... for turned up-so-doun
is al this world ..."
                    —Geoffrey Chaucer, "Lak of Stedfastnesse"

He had the house. A fifty-three year lease,
and in Westminster's sanctuary. Peace.
Safety, he hoped. He had survived before
a government in bloody-minded uproar.

Now friends, already rattled to their bones,
abject and bare-kneed on the cobblestones,
were gasping out their fervid recantations.
No burnings yet, but there were intimations. ...

The old king's man, he mourned the old court's dead.
Could ribald tales in rhyme cost you your head?
(When stories change, who knows where safety is?)
Feeling unsafe, he had retracted his.

Well, he would wait. And what would come would come.

Hereafter, all the documents go dumb,
while from the picture in a gilded book
of *Troilus*, where once John of Gaunt would look
to see the poet reading to a court
in gentle gaiety, in jeweled sport—
all *fin'amor*, all finery, all grace—
some hand has scraped away a dead king's face.

Reassessment

On reading a new biography of Dante

His book? Revenge. Humiliated rage
in terza rima. All his wounded pride
bled from the quill-tip. Nearly every page

was fury, shouted from the losing side
out of his exile, under a threat of death
earned by his vacillating. Now allied

with one mad faction, now straining for breath
to woo the other, jockeying for fame,
move after proud wrong move, he stoked the wrath

that banished him. The book that made his name
hisses an undertext: conniver, toady,
weighing which powers to bless and which to shame.

Fast-forward seven centuries. How odd
that rage now seems to speak the mind of God.

"The best lack all conviction"

On listening to the morning news

Slant light on breakfast dishes. Spring-into-summer
breeze through the screens. And on the radio—
again, again—aubades of war and murder.

Whipped, flailing, a reed in the wind, I throw
my mind in ten directions. What to think?
Finding nothing believable, I shrink
from stepping forward off the granite cliff
of resolution—even while I know
how Dante paints it: wailing tempests blow
to scourge those lukewarm souls who juggle "If"
and "But" and "Still" and "On the other hand . . ."

Convictionless? I am barred from hell and heaven.
Passionate? Cities burn. And who can stand
firm in the firestorm blast that will blow then?

Refuting Marvell

Wrong, friend Andrew. Yes, entirely wrong.
So many, found embracing in the tombs!
Clutching, clasping, spooned or face to face
across millenia:
               In Italy,
the Neolithic lovers of Valdaro
lift fleshless hands to stroke the bones of faces
and twine their legs as if to cling for warmth
under the threadbare blanketing of time.

A dozen pairs of Bronze Age skeletons
locked in the permafrost of Novosibirsk
are posed in the act that their religion teaches
will reconceive them for a second birth.

Two long-limbed men in medieval Kent
lie hip to hip a thousand years, gaped mouths
dark as the age.
               Mostly we find the bones,
the ashes, even, mixed in the urns by strangers.
But once in a great while there comes a gift—

those two in the collapsing factory's rubble
in Bangladesh, his arms circling her waist,
his cheek pressed to her breasts.
                    And though we know
too much about injustice and destruction,
part of the brain goes stubbornly on seeing
his parted lips as adoration, and
the sharp arch of her back as ecstasy.

Myristica fragrans

Common name: nutmeg

Always a bit off balance,
　　　　one stands on a chair, on tiptoe.
Fumbles amid the fragrant small containers.
Shoves the history aside.

One would prefer to forget the great Dutch galleons
　　　　pressing in at the tiny islands of Banda
　　　　and the thin face of Jan Pieterszoon Coen
　　　　framed in a starched ruff.

How he spoke his simple orders.
How the Dutch in their gleaming armor
　　　　drove the young men of Banda over the cliffs.
How their blood scented the water.

How soldiers gathered the native planters together,
　　　　beheading them one by one,
　　　　the heads rotting on pikes, the attar of them
　　　　drifting for days.

How by this means the Dutch East India Company
　　　　savored its luscious success.

One would prefer to forget.
For the Christmas guests are all in the living room, laughing.

And so one taps the jar, and so the eggnog
　　　　is fragrant with this forgetting

and with rum, too, though that is another story.

Universal Vault Fire, 1 June 2008

"Those songs will never be heard again."
—*"The Day the Music Burned,"* New York Times,
11 June 2019

Eleven years ago, they burned. I read the news this morning,
mourned for the nameless gospel choirs and Delta blues this
   morning.

From the court documents, the losses smolder like doused ruins:
years of top-forty rock that my brain keeps rattling loose this
   morning. . . .

After the first death, the poet sang, *there is no other*
but this, worse than the mangled airplane, the pills and booze
   this morning.

Archetypes of our joy, our rage, consumed in oily smoke—
How irresistibly the world has turned its screws this morning.

Where did they go, my waist-length hair, my Dreadnought-body
   Martin,
my songs of revolution? What is my excuse this morning?

My name is no excuse. Will music ever save the world
from universal burning? How much more will we lose this
   morning?

"Massacre of Children in Peru Might Have Been a Sacrifice to Stop Bad Weather"

—New York Times, *6 March 2019*

We, of course, will develop other approaches.
Before the great evil descends and the sea devours the cities,
before the unbearable rains dissolve the hillsides
into a slurry of mud that falls away,
dragging with it the wealth of our charming suburbs,
we will take more effective measures.
We will certainly not be found
binding our children's hands, leading our sacred llamas,
half-marching and half-dragging them
(the beasts bawling, the children perhaps drugged senseless)
through the destroying mud, to the killing fields
where priests complete the bloody, desperate work
of offering to the gods our most precious treasure.
Possessing more enlightened techniques,
we will have no need for ritual mass burial
and for smearing skulls with cinnabar mixed with our tears.

Our young are differently marked,
marked by the gaze of policemen armed for slaughter.
Already we are recording them, the methods
used by our priests for extraction of the heart.

In Code

For my old colleagues, who write the words of the law

Ours is a stunted tongue,
    mostly unmouthed, rarely licked into life.

In it, one may not exclaim,
    wonder, or boast. Threats
    are common, though. Laughter
    is illicit, poetry impossible.

This language mutters its orders
    in Miltonic auxiliary verbs,

shall and *shall not*, repeating
    the cadences of Leviticus,

nervously listing (1) particulars,
    (2) specifics, (3) details, and
    (4) cloudy mumblings.

Most utterances are stillborn.
    The few that live lie breathless, with folded hands.

We gather them into the volumes
    we hope they do not speak.

They bind us tightly, like wounds.

Riddle 40: Pen in Hand

From the Old English of the Exeter Book

I saw four beings   beautifully fashioned
traveling together.   Their track was a dark one,
the path quite black.   Swift was its passing.
Livelier than birds,   it luffed in air
and dived beneath waves.   The doughty warrior
who led them all forward   labored unflagging
to guide the four   over beaten gold.

Stone Ground

After meeting an old classmate at a technical writing conference

The manuals for heart and lung machines,
the indexes for case and statute books—
that's what we write now. *Refugees*, he called us,
from English programs. Somehow, we've escaped
(our ears still full of *Not by bread alone*)
alive, out to the world, where plain-cut words
are stone enough to build a life that stands.

We take our poems now in single bites:
scruff-haired, still in our robes, we squint at screens.
A poem a day, each morning's spare devotion.
The gift there, held before us like a host,
says, *Take and eat. Do this in memory*.
We chew, swallow, resolve to change our lives,
then head across the yards, out to the cars,
off to the coarse-grained world. We wait for grace,
the grit of stony crust against our teeth.

A Volume of Cases

The stiff-sewn quires. The buckram cover.
The meth abuse. The absent mother.
The prepaid phones that called each other.

The home foreclosed. The groaning debt.
The liabilities offset.
The punch thrown in the bar. The threat.

The dry recitals, where and when.
The last appeals of dying men.
The sentence to be parsed again.

The deference. The court's respect.
The reasoning it must reject.
The lives behind the pages, wrecked.

The pieces that will not align.
The silent matters they decline.
The gold impressed into the spine.

Working Draft

This poem incorporates by reference
the little winces of my working life,

the years of small regrets.

For purposes of this poem, "regrets"
shall mean and shall include without limitation:

the movements of a pen on paper, which
quietly but with absolute precision,
made lives invisible,

the neat strikeouts of phrases, which undid
a hundred constituent letters,
a thousand protesters chanting,

the zig and zag of lines on certain maps,
which sentenced them to decades without voices,

the guilty knowledge of these gains, those losses,
guarded by a professional ambience
formally classified as hazardous
by all the applicable federal standards.

This poem shall be construed
to give effect to its intent: mixed feelings,
a plain meaning, for which
no court's interpretation is required.

Praise Ode to the Customer Service Agent

Blessings on her, the actual human voice
I reach after mechanic eons on hold,
saccharine soft-rock dribbling in my ear.

Hear how carefully, carefully she attends
first to my voice, the pitch of furious patience,
the pull, precise along the vocal folds,
in which I almost crack with fear and worry.
She does not interrupt. Worthy of the stage
is the skill with which she brings the script alive,
the gentle drawl soothing its parchment grammar
to guide my panicked breathing into slowness,
the easy containment that does not betray
her fatigue, her boredom, or her pent-up longing
to clock out here and get to her second job.

Blessings even upon the whipped-cream smoothness
in which she must announce the special offers.

May I remember how the electrons lilt
with blessing when I click the evaluation,
which will arrive by e-mail in three minutes
to sum this little drama in all its scenes
(its questions numbered, choices one to ten).

Let no one hold it like a knife to her throat.

The Vanished

In the autumn of 2015, the production of paper cards for library catalogs ceased.

No matter how long ago they completed their disappearance,
    I still expect them,
perhaps in a sort of narthex just past a pillared entry,
    or off to the side
as if in a private chapel, or straight ahead like an altar.
    Shrined in the silence,
modest and single, or ranged in ranks and banks and rows,
    the gods of Order
lived in their tabernacles of honey and amber maple
    or oak like chocolate,
darkened at times from the touch of a hundred thousand fingers.
    On every drawer-front
the face of a tiny gargoyle waggled its brazen tongue out.
    And so we pulled them.
And the drawers slid waxen-smooth, and the fingers flicked like a weaver's
    through card upon card,
and above the drawers were our faces, our heads bobbing and davening.
    A kind of worship
it was, with an order of service. A physical act of obeisance.
    Its cloudy replacement
(perfect in plastic efficiency, answering almost to thought,
    near-disembodied)
hurries us past the notion of order itself as a Being
    worthy of honor.
So here I am, misplaced as a balky fourth-century pagan
    mulling conversion,
but nursing doubts that the powers should be called from the general air;
    seeking the numinous
still in its tent of presence, and longing to keep on clutching
    the household gods.

The Indexers Talk Back to Borges

Of a certain minor poet of the Greek Anthology, Borges wrote,
You are a word in an index.

In the rapt evenings that turned too soon to night,
we have sat, in ancient days, at dining-room tables
with index cards, with old shoeboxes, with galleys.
Listen, Jorge Luis! We mean to unsay you:

that poet you mourn as though his only memorial
were dust, his verses flaked into vellum fragments—
we with our slips of paper, blue pencils, typewriters
have set him as carefully down on a slender column
(two to a page, crammed into six-point type)
as a name in granite cut by a carver's chisel.

We led the way to the page where your pity found him
and grieved his meager remnants, his nightingale's singing.
Mark this—mark chiefly this, Jorge!—you found him
because of us, and our care, and our quiet sorting
with the light leaning across our kitchen counters
through winter evenings, or in at the blinds of summer
on mornings when cardinals' song was a pour of honey.

We have marked his place forever. Remember us, Jorge—
though the gods have seemed ungenerous to us also—
now that old ways are withered. The slips of paper
sift into dustless electrons. The dry workspaces
are lit by screens. The songs of digital birds
repeat, repeat from the tinny hearts of the speakers.

Reasons for Hesitation

Because I've sized you up—I, puny biped;
    you, in your motorized Gargantua,

Because I wait in my flimsy human frame
    for the walk signal, shivering and stamping
    in the late-winter morning's mingy twilight,

Because I hear the morning's gunning motor—
    the drive chain of its oversize ambition,
    the insect-whine of rumors in a hallway,
    old worries idling, dirtying the air,

Because, against these forces, my soul's value
    is zero absolutely, given the windchill
    across that patch of ice now glittering
    between your wheeled behemoth and my crosswalk,

Because I've read the news that my coworker
    (she of the bright red hair and ready smile
    at the reception desk) is dead this morning
    of a grave error: rummaging through her purse
    for something that was not the approaching train,

Because the engine of some nameless will
    tosses us through our days as helplessly
    as her red shoe, shown in the photograph,
    still lying in the street.

A Personal Account

I think of it—the money I've put away—
as sitting primly, waiting to be called on,
wearing a plaid jumper and saddle shoes
and bobby socks. It keeps its ankles crossed.

I know it's not like that. I'm not naïve.
The money doesn't sit. It's lent. It does things,
I don't know what. Lately it's out of touch.
We've never talked about its private life.

So if my money's been out partying
in dives, in sleazy places I wouldn't approve of,
draped on the arm of an oily, fat-ass banker
and dressed like a tramp, with too much makeup on,

don't tell me. Please. I do not want to know.
It can come home, and all will be forgiven.

Fearful for my government job, dreaming of retirement, I think of Du Fu

Headline: "President Looks to Slash Nearly 4000 Interior Department Jobs"
—NPR

Tell me, venerable poet, how did you cope
with changes of regime?

Did you listen, in the gardens of Chang'an,
while men in new silk robes
spoke your name and snickered?

Did they practice, in their graceful calligraphy,
the characters for *cutting the fat?*
For *starving the beast?*

Did you watch as others suffered,
like you, demotion and disgrace?

You, too, longed for peace,
for a farm, a thatched cottage, the sound of a stream.

Teach me how you mastered yourself
to leave us poems worth these thousand years
of rivers, moonlight, compassion.

Teach me how you knew it was time at last
to flee before the barbarians.

A Room at the Student Union

Recalled on Armistice Day, 2018

It's bright and tidy, if a little lacking
in the amenities. And blessedly warm
after a slog through early-winter snow
from the Megabus, in a blue darkness falling
slantwise across the Midwest-campus flatness.
Two lamps, one chair. Thank God, a private bath;
a single bed made up with barrack strictness.
Spartan. That word's associations flash
to what the place-name means: *Memorial* Union.
The bronze plaque in the entryway announced them,
the dead, in a hundred years of green patina
that salves the memory.

                But the world's still broken.
How do I mend it, staring from my window
high above campus, in the meager dusk?
The poetry I'm here to read mends nothing,
merely piecing the breakage into beauty.
I squint out to the foursquare, old-world order
(revival Romanesque in local stone)
where the last vestige of the day-class schedule
is a few student bodies bent to the wind.
Oblivious to a century's brokenness,
they keep the quad's straight paths, walled in by the snow,
their life plans, and the dead weight of the sky.

Shall I beg God to let them go on bending
in peace? To turn the pages of the Norton
untroubled, past *our quarrel with the foe*
and the Old Lie of *dulce et decorum*
in perfect ignorance of what it means,
"memorial union"? That's what I almost pray for
this evening, as the carillon's holy bells
summon the place to something not quite prayer,
clanging "Imagine" as a vespers hymn.

Sleep, Loss

Once past the pang of handing in her keys,
she met none of the miseries foretold
for the retired. Those bus-stop waits in the cold
were well lost, and she slept the sleep of peace
alarmless. What dawned slowly was a dulled
or loosened hold on morning's luxuries—
the moon, a sliced pearl set in lapis skies
diamonded by one planet, with the gold-
red band of sunrise chasing her.
                                    And she thought
then of an older loss: when her last child
had learned to sleep till daylight, and her lulled
limbs fled communion with the monk, the night-
watcher, the graveyard shift, as she became
an outcast from the house of two a.m.

An Ancient in First-Year Greek

Well, yes, it's odd.
Past sixty-five, and grayer than a Sistine-ceiling God,

mildly I face the board, among
these shining-faced and slightly nervous young,

bumbling along with them, in kindergarten lisp and stammer
through bafflements of grammar

and strange opacities of alphabet.
Already I think their shoulders slump a bit beneath their debt,

but in this room, we equally ignore
the susurration of the rising sea, the roar

of Syrian bombers, the drowned children on the beaches,
the looming dark-age misery that teaches

despair and skull-numbed fear.
But here, here

we are, poor dreamers, laboring at the lore
of tongues that have seen the world collapse before

and that will know, when it comes crashing down, when dire
becomes most dire,
old stories, good to chant around a fire.

Notes

"Threats" on page 3: The Alfred P. Murrah Building was bombed on 19 April 1995 in a domestic terrorist attack. The bombing killed 168 people.

"Capitol café" on page 6 refers to the German-themed Rathskeller Café in the basement of the Minnesota State Capitol.

"Poses" on page 10 refers to the statues of Floyd B. Olson, Charles Lindbergh, and Hubert Humphrey on the Minnesota Capitol mall.

"Map of the Ten Thousand Countries of the World" on page 15: Matteo Ricci was an Italian Jesuit missionary to China in the early seventeenth century. With his famous map, he introduced the Chinese to European ideas of the shape of the world and the universe.

"Open Verdict" on page 19: An open verdict, in the British system, is a verdict of a coroner's jury that does not reach a conclusion about the cause of a death.

"Ninety Seconds of News Coverage at 6 P.M." on page 26: The Minnesota State Capitol's marble facade had been deteriorating for decades before it was finally restored in 2015–2017.

"A Diplomatic Post" on page 41: The French poet Joachim du Bellay spent the years from 1553 to 1557 as a diplomat in Italy.

"Creed" on page 42: A popular account of the history behind this poem can be found in Richard Rubenstein's *When Jesus Became God*.

"December 1399" on page 54: Though no one knows how Geoffrey Chaucer died, Terry Jones's book *Who Murdered Chaucer?* makes the case that his unorthodox religious views could have led to his end after the death of Richard II.

"Refuting Marvell" on page 57 refers to the last stanza of the poem "To His Coy Mistress" and to a photograph of two of the dead in the 2013 collapse of the Rana Plaza building near Dhaka, Bangladesh. The accident killed more than a thousand people.

"Riddle 40: Pen in Hand" on page 62: The "four beings" are the pen and the three fingers that hold it; the warrior is the arm that moves them all. "Beaten gold" might refer to the inkhorn point or possibly to the gold of illuminations.

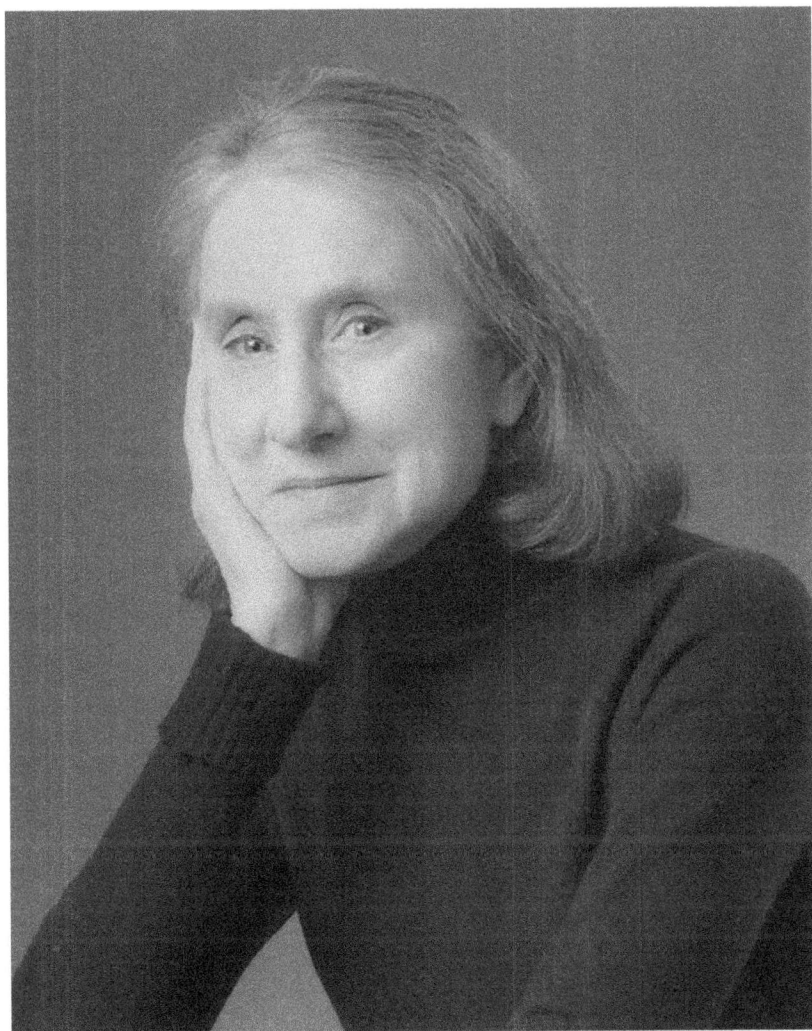

MARYANN CORBETT earned a doctorate in English in 1981, with a specialization in medieval literature and linguistics. She expected to be teaching *Beowulf* and Chaucer and the history of the English language. Instead, she spent almost thirty-five years working for the Minnesota Legislature, helping attorneys to write in plain English and coordinating the creation of finding aids for the law.

She is the author of five books of poetry and is a past winner of the Richard Wilbur Award and the Willis Barnstone Translation Prize. Her work is widely published in journals on both sides of the Atlantic and is included in anthologies like *Measure for Measure: An Anthology of Poetic Meters* and *The Best American Poetry 2018.*

ALSO FROM ABLE MUSE PRESS

Richard Newman, *All the Wasted Beauty of the World* – Poems

Alfred Nicol, *Animal Psalms* – Poems

Deirdre O'Connor, *The Cupped Field (Able Muse Book Award for Poetry)*

Frank Osen, *Virtue, Big as Sin (Able Muse Book Award for Poetry)*

Alexander Pepple (Editor), *Able Muse Anthology;*
Able Muse – a review of poetry, prose & art (semiannual, winter 2010 on)

James Pollock, *Sailing to Babylon* – Poems

Aaron Poochigian, *The Cosmic Purr* – Poems;
Manhattanite (Able Muse Book Award for Poetry)

Tatiana Forero Puerta, *Cleaning the Ghost Room* – Poems

Jennifer Reeser, *Indigenous* – Poems

John Ridland, *Sir Gawain and the Green Knight (Anonymous)* – Translation;
Pearl (Anonymous) – Translation

Stephen Scaer, *Pumpkin Chucking* – Poems

Hollis Seamon, *Corporeality* – Stories

Ed Shacklee, *The Blind Loon: A Bestiary*

Carrie Shipers, *Cause for Concern (Able Muse Book Award for Poetry)*

Matthew Buckley Smith, *Dirge for an Imaginary World* (*Able Muse Book Award for Poetry*)

Susan de Sola, *Frozen Charlotte* – Poems

Barbara Ellen Sorensen, *Compositions of the Dead Playing Flutes* – Poems

Rebecca Starks, *Time Is Always Now* – Poems
Fetch Muse – Poems

Sally Thomas, *Motherland* – Poems

J.C. Todd, *Beyond Repair* – Poems

Paulette Demers Turco (Editor), *The Powow River Poets Anthology II*

Rosemerry Wahtola Trommer, *Naked for Tea* – Poems

Wendy Videlock, *Slingshots and Love Plums* – Poems;
The Dark Gnu and Other Poems;
Nevertheless – Poems

Richard Wakefield, *A Vertical Mile* – Poems
Terminal Park – Poems

Gail White, *Asperity Street* – Poems

Chelsea Woodard, *Vellum* – Poems

Rob Wright, *Last Wishes* – Poems

www.ablemusepress.com